# DRY STONED WALLS

## Paul Evans

# DRY STONED WALLS

## Poems on Alcohol Addiction, Recovery, and Connection with the Welsh Landscape

*Paul Evans*

*Onion Custard Publishing Ltd*

# Dry Stoned Walls
*Poems on Alcohol Addiction, Recovery, and Connection*
*with the Welsh Landscape*

British Library Cataloguing in Publication Data. A catalogue record for this book is available from the British Library.

Published in the United Kingdom by Onion Custard Publishing Ltd.
www.onioncustard.com
Twitter @onioncustard
Facebook.com/OnionCustardPublishing

Paperback: ISBN: 9781911265078

First Edition: February, 2016
Category: Poetry

For Jacqui

# Table of Contents

Introduction ....................................................... 1

What Price? ....................................................... 4

Walking it off .................................................... 5

Recovering Souls ................................................ 6

Salmon in Moray ................................................ 8

Doubt Dominated ............................................... 9

Recall ............................................................. 10

Forgiveness ..................................................... 12

Liquorice Wine ................................................. 13

Hamlet Too ...................................................... 14

George ........................................................... 16

Neuadd .......................................................... 17

Never in a Drinking Dream ................................. 18

Crags ............................................................. 19

Marinas .......................................................... 20

Tommy ........................................................... 21

Dawkins et. al. ................................................. 22

Loose Stones ................................................... 24

Heron ............................................................ 25

A Stone's Throw ............................................... 26

Leaving Rehab .................................................. 27

Resentment and Gratitude ................................. 28

Returning ....................................................... 29

Even Now ........................................................ 30

Graves' Web ..................................................... 32

I Frightened Them ...................................................... 33

Patrisio ................................................................... 34

School Yard Select ..................................................... 35

Stalker .................................................................... 36

Stay off it ................................................................ 37

Swan ...................................................................... 38

Straight the Way ....................................................... 39

The Blank Page ......................................................... 40

Taff ....................................................................... 41

The Lion .................................................................. 42

Faith....................................................................... 48

Dad ....................................................................... 44

Mam....................................................................... 46

# Introduction

*Who has woe? Who has sorrow?*
*Who has strife? Who has complaints?*
*Who has needless bruises? Who has bloodshot eyes?*
*Those who linger over wine,*
*Who go to sample bowls of mixed wine.*
*Do not gaze at wine when it is red,*
*When it sparkles in the cup,*
*When it goes down smoothly!*
*In the end it bites like a snake*
*And poisons like a viper.*
*Your eyes will see strange sights*
*And your mind imagine confusing things.*
*You will be like one sleeping on the high seas*
*Lying on top of the rigging.*
*"They hit me," you will say, "but I'm not hurt!*
*They beat me up, but I don't feel it!*
*When will I wake up*
*So I can find another drink!"*

**Proverbs**

I was astonished to find this vivid description of alcoholism in the 23rd Proverb of the Old Testament. Revelation indeed to find my condition so acutely observed some one thousand years before the birth of Christ.

Alcohol slithered into my life; a thief of time, purpose, and self-respect. While the illness produced an intense craving and a profound obsession with the vile stuff, my return to health is demonstrating how lasting change *is* possible by surrendering to the very powers that held me in the chains of the status quo.

In this sense, my recovery from addiction has been a spiritual experience as well as an emotional and physical one. My dependence went beyond the base physical alcoholic need. A lifelong reliance on external sources for peace and happiness, coupled with an ingrained sense of entitlement to health and wellbeing, led to complacency on the one hand, and a deep need to control everything and everyone around me on the other.

The continuity of landscape features prominently in my work, particularly as it contrasts the more transient aspects of our constructed lives and environments. Recovery has been about waking up and growing up. Images of struggle and awakening in the natural world resonate therefore.

I acknowledge my direct references to C.S. Lewis in "The Lion", and William Nicholson in "Walking It Off", where I quote briefly from *Shadowlands*. I draw on the soliloquies of a fellow prevaricator in "Hamlet Too" and there are nods of homage to Dylan Thomas and Gerard Manley Hopkins along the way. Robert Graves' *The Cool Web* has been a lasting influence; language created the masks I wore to make my "retreat from too much joy and too much fear" and my poem reflects his marvellous work. I trust my style and content is my own, but should there be inadvertent references or allusions to other writers, I gladly acknowledge them.

I would like to thank all at Onion Custard for their guidance and support in bringing this collection to print and to express my deepest gratitude to family and friends for their love and encouragement. Finally, I owe my life and this work to the fellowship of a 12-step recovery programme.

# What Price?

What price a blindness
Too proud to shorten sail
Into barreled storms?

Oaks twig break in swell;
Rum bloods the bone cage shore
Under fleeing skies.

Foundered on bullion rocks;
Seamanship overboard
In grey swirl moonshine.

Schooner shifts on ebb
Of rudderless rigging.
Beached mast heads resign

Slow sand gathering
Anchors to cellared sea
Bottle burial.

Lettered tides send home
Flotsam and jetsam rolls
Of a dishonour

Crewed in brute hubris.
Gulled auguries gather
At the gnawing wake.

# Walking it off

Walking it off in the light cold of day,
White streams and mossed stone walls
Appearing just for me in this torrential downtime,
New year not yet beckoning
In this waiting room of the world time
Spawned in beacons' shadowlands.
Pen-y-fan hanging in wet shroud
Descends into Neuadd's swirling
As Dolygaer and Ponsticill become one
In this deepness of days.
Farms beyond ruin steam still
In drowned valleys dammed for graceless cities.
Landscape claims them risen,
Making natural the made,
Where in deeper forest,
Spraying the silence of a dry stone past
The falls sing proud in their secret tumbling.

# Recovering Souls

Recovering souls searching truth
Through the tales from a heart of dark
In rooms where ageless drying youth
Pinpoints essences of its part

In every blacked-out common cause.
Experiential rock bottoms,
Where any time and purpose pause
As nothing may be forgotten

That never was etched in veiled mind;
For similarity mirrors,
In crannied, shadowed, wounded kind,
An awful sameness of rivers.

Belligerent and aggressive
Fallings of early indulgence
Down the bottle-necked oppressive
Denial of every instance

You drank into another face.
Alcohol swollen breakage:
A spiritless absence of grace
The inevitable leakage

Dripping respect and tenderness.
A dissolution of compass
In liquid single-mindedness.
Evolutionary Thymus -

Leaving us to our own device.
A compromised immunity
Where in spiritual progress
Clarities emerge stumblingly.

# Salmon in Moray

In flows green by your youthful river
I watch your speckled journeys converge.
Through the stone-dappled transparency
You rise in the natural weir.

Late this day in the Black Isle beyond
Dolphin-boated Moray morning crest,
Above quilt gold in its quiet resting,
Along this midge mist lochside mooring

You shift into Highland, as sand swirls
Become shallow and you settle to
Pebbled remembrance of homecoming,
Rippling in your birthing eloquence.

Bones in walls and forests testament
To our oneness across time and sea;
You build a moss fern future
On the cusp of our secret waters.

Quiet inside, they dream of homeland.
As I drift to your stilling stream
Laying my toes furtive in your world
I raise my eyes to your guiding stars.

# Doubt Dominated

Doubt dominated the hollow day,
Echoes tinny in their returning emptiness.
The routine response of bottled ease
Cushioned evenings in mute denial
Of the shallowness,
Physical in its presenting need.
Alcohol's warm smooth gratifying offer
To target the strained solar plexus,
Accepted in assuaging instant.
Guttural joy delivered in deep swallowed
Diaphragm loosening thirst wiping waves
Driving deeper need for immediacy in all comfort,
In progressive dependence
On sordid places and things.
Suicidal surrender inevitable; its eventual emergence
In the latent light of willingness
The catalyst to lasting change.
Colour, fuller and deeper the autumnal fruit,
Admission cornerstones the arch,
Choice returns on the swollen river of a recovered soul,
Forgiveness removes dams in the high valleys,
And beyond, where the echoes return rounded
And dry stone walls circle the holy pools,
We wait in sacramental reflection.
Doing for us what we could not do for ourselves,
Open mind, willingness, and honesty
Work a practical trinity; triangular protection
From the first and fatal sip.
Yet more in mellow sleep,
In wakeful acceptance of life's uneasy terms.

# Recall

Excruciating thread between betterness
Pulled gullet-tight down the crow craw
And abdication's loose handshake.
Easy daytime televisual solace;
Responsibility withdraws
Lilting free on the welching wake.
Life's weights lifted from the unwilling shoulder,
Merely hallucinations' haul
In the haze green bottle day.
Consciousness, the low cloud against a grey scape,
Leaves little trace passing through
On its faceless, graceless way.
You drift beyond my focus, caring for me,
Wiping up after more spilled hope;
Blood staining carpeted terror.
You capture me fetal round the belching bowl
Positioned for posterity
In another en suite horror.
Ill-fitting stones fill my retrospective view
Down the telescope barrel sky
Of amnesic constellations.
My reliance on your clear present story
Frustrates you beyond imagining
In half-measure consolation.
For memory's absence is not the issue
As I grope for understanding
In your pain and patient recall.

More the failure to step outside the image,
To turn round; to see what you saw
Of my dark, spiritless downfall.
Ever seeing what I could not in myself
You stayed for the plastered promise
Barely twinkling in my hateful
Eyes only for the blackout-beckoning night.
You stayed 'til I breathed of morning;
Reached for the soul bottle grateful.
Acceptance that assumptions should never suffice;
We can never know what we felt
Before a recovery grew.
Understanding may rise in self's removing,
Listening left in pride's empty seat,
Love's continuing all we knew.

# Forgiveness

Forgiveness and forgetting strain at resentment's leash;
Tug-o-Warred status quo.
Lift your bagged red eyes to the quiet un-judging hills.
You may gently let go
Of the past's hold.

Eye similarity; for to sniff the difference
In status or stories,
A crude collusion in wine's indifferent circling.
Saviour's hand sorely
Rejected by self's haste.

Spiritual practicality; today's offer.
Choose your own God in fact.
High-powered options in a self-build awakening
To breach the poisoned pact
With the Devil's water.

Cunning, confusing, patient, its grip you remember
As red and golden ease.
Past the knife wrist morning of a planned and fitting end,
Partner to strong ripe cheese,
It's sacramental pull.

# Liquorice Wine

No mild anaesthetic,
Nor social lubricant sipped in guileful pose.
Avoiding pubescent boozy nights post-sport
In the white lightness;
Control evaporating in toxic flair.
A weightlessness of crystal confidence
Where hold slips along wine's smooth rounded softness
Behind curtain-pull evenings.
When the momentary ease
Was discovered like a thief in the night who wanted to chat,
I introduced my father to cheap Cabernet.
Tumbler connoisseurs in eloquence eluding sunset;
Pretention's slurry portend of dementia's stroll.
But alcohol was in me announcing its intention
To be in for the long haul.
*Tastes like the black stuff in* Liquorice All Sorts, he pondered,
Raising his wistful glass to the half-cut moon.

# Hamlet Too

That this oh too solid flesh would melt too
In the scarring rain.
How hollow resolution overdue
Could remove the stain.

To live or not to live in life's dark thrall
Of dependent guile.
I fled Him down an empty sky fall
Of yellowing bile.

To lay, dying for a want of dreaming;
Consummation's flaw.
I hid in the vaulted viscous steaming
Of death's chyle-full craw.

I fled the unremembered conceit.
Bacchus-livered days,
Feeding free of the o'er flowing teat
On his slothful chaise.

To laugh at the oppressors' shouting.
Outrageous riches
I fled You; spurned You in my snouting
Dance of the ditches.

I fled You in the deep sinuses,
In my pothole fears.
I fled You in the dark silences
Of agnostic sneers.

How to hold a mirror to the face
Of this peasant rogue?
Surrender to your relentless grace,
Fall into the drogue

You hold in the wake of my tumult
Breaking my ghost fall
Your steadfast followings I exult.
Hold me in your Welsh shawl

And whisper to thine own self be true.
Nature's steadiness,
One day at a time willingness grew.
All is readiness.

# George

You tubed in legion hits,
More than goals the tackles ridden and won.
Creation the essence
In legendary shift from boy to man
On a winger's toes,
Out of nothing in the beautiful game
Jewelled by your running rings.
Along fitful public end your balance
Dipped in remembering,
I never imagined emulation would present
In second chance and broken promise.
Perhaps I know when your first champagne
In those heady seasons
Spoke to a kid's winsome destiny
Beyond the loose-stoned yard.
In the vile grip of the bubbles' eyes
You strode street and stadium.
Held in the rigging, horizons never came
To the boy with the world at his feet
And scars on his liver.
I thought you might ride one last tackle
On a bylined wing to your terraced glory.

# Neuadd

In sharp night over Tal-y-Bont
Deep white is brooding Pen-y-fan
Holding the silent cut glass falls
In its veined and ancient limestone.

Kites no longer valleyed secrets
Lift on morning's supple soaring,
Forked gold in steepening beacon,
Gliders of the Spring-hungry Glyn.

Bleak art in the stillness of stone.
Whimsical grass shoots through,
Cutting white gold in winter frame,
Flaked slow in its subtle sculpting.

Views sweep screed through Llangynidr,
Thrown down on yacht winded Llangorse
To ancient tracks beyond Brecon
And the dry stone walls of the North.

In its mid-life meandering
Usk beckons the streaming children;
Come with my muddy maturing
To the welcoming new port sea.

# Never in a Drinking Dream

Never in drinking dream,
Nor under the golden apples of a tree full birth
Was communion's wineless goblet
Or bread's crust calling.
Shallowness gripped.
In reprieve's contingent awakening
Dependence dissolves,
As once moral resolve,
Facing vine's temptful summons.
Acceptance the wardrobe key;
Patience suffocated in want's furs.
Relieved of the indulgence of self,
Contentment unfurls;
One's own role the only truth
In the street-sweeping daybreak.
As future's twigs snap in the dry light
Of realignment - past's poison pours empty
Down the precious bottles of the burgeoning
Open mind, and a willing perspective returns
On forgiving wings through a prideless sky.
Pillowed sleep restless only for the sober dawn.

# Crags

Steep narrow trails and loose rock,
Knuckle white escarpments driving eyes to earth,
Drying mud laced tight;
Imaginary toes dipped in drinking streams.
Rucksack sweats;
Soft finger map and compass to hand
In this new landscape.
Legged heavy vales cleaner in their promise
Invite different views.
Ancient toxicity drawn out like peat,
Cut through pores in the high meadow
As trails emerge from the feral firs;
In the cradling crags
The muddied falls carry my blood transfused
Down the rivers of the crest fall night
To the waiting grace-filled sea.

# Marinas

Avoiding prurient balcony bland
And the champagne cruisers gliding glib
Bullying older ships in their rot wood mooring,
I held my gaze on the young man
Working on the steamer,
Sanding life into the *African Queen*;
Sawdust deck gleaning his prints,
She awaits the first coat
Patient whenever he may come
In his self-forgetting toil,
One day at a time.
Untying the craft that brings him,
He glances my way and I raise a glass
In envious recognition of his timeless acceptance.
He nods and drifts away
In the low sun on the monied water,
Home in the wake of another sail-tinkling night.

# Tommy

One of those anonymous Welshmen;
To cry laughing when he walked on.
The familiarity.
Fezzed master clown,
Square jaw and watery setback eye
Tapping into our daily ineptitude,
Masked in the magic circling of our collective love.
Perceiving the brilliance hidden,
Just like that
In the deepness of the illusion.
Delusion shards, on and off stage
In the sodden handkerchief drama
Played out to the adoring in a myriad impressions,
Never quite capturing the flawed and easy genius
Somehow at the heart of all me meant to me.

# Dawkins et. al.

Dawkins, Dennett, Harris, and Hitchens
Would have you believe I'm deluded.
With Lewis, Spufford, McGrath, and Williams
I've consciously colluded.
I don't believe it took a week,
Nor every word in the Book.
As long as science sticks to its brief
I'll always take a look
At the proof it ever claims to breed
To face down religious patter
But really, guys, in quantum please,
What is this deep dark matter?
Because the odds of being here
Prod answers more divine,
You invent the myth of the multiverse;
Intelligent design
Indeed - another *Star Trek* story,
Where evidence seems quite spurious.
The lords of the great enlightenment
Would have been, I'm sure, quite furious.
In your secular science and arrogant pomp
My faith you attempt to trounce,
Yet your latest incarnation
Is the joke of the Great Big Bounce.
As science falters at the starting point
Of how it came to be
The Big Bang can't explain away
A sense of eternity.
In the *New Scientist* just last week
Some stories untoward.

How they haven't explained how we balance a bike
Or why time will always be forward.
My faith in the end will stand or fall
On the strength of my own experience;
Not on the gaps in the secular surge
To blind my belief through science.
The Gospels are not just gospel to me
For historians are not always right,
But the authors were writing close to the time
When the Word became the Light.
And how could a man so zealous a Jew
That he held their coats while they murdered
Be blinded by truth on a dusty road
And within years had travelled and furthered
The words of the man who hung on the cross
For political insurrection,
Dead and buried with his scurrilous claims
Burst free at his resurrection?
And if to the court of *The Brights* I'm brought
To prove my discovery,
I'll point to the drunk in the guttered grime
Then his recovery.
For there I see with balanced eye
The evidence unrehearsed
Of a life reborn in God's one earth,
No need for a multiverse.

# Loose Stones

Grit hard-picked from thumb's fleshy base
In needle mothered first aid.
Court and field our dingle drive;
Floodlit gravelled games
Under helter grey hail fall.
Stone melt skinful nights
Out black of the shelterless reckoning.
Wrung in attestable fear,
A vaultiness requiring deeper surgery
Submits to the storm gathering.
Two hearts blind to loftier tunes,
Self-strung on passion's hoar light -
Perspective whelmed under the mortgaged soul.
Simple instruction spurned
To found the structure on loose stones.

# Heron

Your twig neck dips to the lichen lake,
Stilt grey perch on slow moss wood drift.
Natural art in your balanced eye,
Needle-mouthed singularity
At the prey full banks' sober silence.
Sharp pleasure in your talon eyeline;
Your harpoon head from the fisher's shore
Pikes deep in the silver rainbow skin.
Lithe response to her hungry nesting
You tilt full, triumphant to her calling,
Then rise - a grey and feathered cross
Breaking loud the fishbone morning.
You bank across the sun-lift sky
Above the heron haunted marshes.

# A Stone's Throw

A stone's throw up the valley
We played above the cloud after the rain
Running our schoolyard day over the loose stones.
Little we knew of the generation-removing slurry
Sliding off its sodden hill into the classrooms.
As we reached for the sky they reached for a hand.
Men dug in the stuff they'd dug before.
Now I walk the stone lines,
Tendered still in their pristine remembrance
And they sing proud of the morning,
When I was so close and yet so far.

# Leaving Rehab

When I left rehab again,
Sun on my back,
Eyes opened in the *Librium* light,
The weakness in my arms and the shakes
Took many dreams to ease
In the beds of lost time and spite-filled rage;
Blacked out, hard shouldered,
Death inviting madness
With my son in the back.
Breakdown of life marred in want;
Perspective drowned in sodden self-esteem,
Swept away on tsunamis of broken promises.
I know you had to leave when you did.
Measure, I still remember nothing of when I was ugliest.
Neighbours stirred and shaken
To express concern through paper walls.
And still I watched in morbid doubt
Your every move and glance.
I saw the removal vans through the bottle bottom,
The men step over me against a fleeting sky.
Awake to the blue siren again and a tube in my arm.
You were gone, a son returned prodigal
To a frightened fold.

# Resentment
# and Gratitude

Resentment and gratitude uneasy bedfellows
In hostels of dry sobriety.
Un-oiled feeling creaks open, gaping tender
In renewed society.
Faith in an old friend transplanted by fear:
Cirrhotic consequence
Driving amended need in want of memories
And restored eloquence.
Assumption and easy, soft apologetics suffice
As bases of truth.
Blythe spiritual progress claims my knowing
Role in your youth.
Uneducated, this variety of awakening demands
Your attention
To my clear and present improved perspective.
My intention
To wipe my slate with the rag of your forgiveness,
As I am sane.
Arrogant delusion my complacent acknowledgment
Of your pain.
Parental rights swept away on crests of ranted rage;
Blacked out crimes
Recurrent in the alcoholic stones weighing
On lost time.

# Returning

Down the dust-lung pit at fourteen.
Forging age to walk to war
On legs made strong at the face.
One blown away in winter furrow;
Stunt sealed in deep-frosted youth
Held still in this shrapnelled place.
Ammonite crater in your hand
And black hole in your shoulder.
Nerve full stump of sawbone cry,
Woollen sock, string, leather-strapped
Comfort in the smooth tight joints
Of hinged and exchangeable thigh.
Your crutch-swung remembrance leaving
The poppy parades in rage
To those medaled colours intact
At cenotaph-grey mornings.
You returned to french field ahead of sleep,
Awe circling your silent knowing pact;
Here in memory-seeded church,
Where so close to the end,
In scarred and crumbling respite,
You sang with the Rhondda boy
Playing organ in the shell fall
Of a welsh remembered night.

# Even Now

Even now I feel it,
And no wine has glazed oesophageal varices
Or stirred a swollen spleen for some years.
One day at a time I travel away from the last drink,
Ever closer to the next
The cynic observes at arm's length.
As far as I may ever be from the first
That kills;
Drawing me in and drink driving me on
In unassuageable craving and obsessive heart;
Such imposters clawing deep in the scarring
For what is and will be until the blackness falls.
To wake in the cave of the bottle-monsters
Who syphon those you stored
For the emergency of consciousness.
Horror mornings when the drink is gone
And the shops are closed,
And the strewn garden bottles,
Lost vessels of thrown dreams call.
If I crawl in the mud and lie in the leaves
I may find comfort in the thorns;
A slurp, in the slime genie's
Wish-granting momentary ease,
Until the taxi reaches the Grail
That now takes credit cards, thank God,
And I drink over the bottle.
If only.

I stop shaking and he pulls over so I can vomit.
I drink again and keep it down.
I drink again and follow with an empty swallow.
I can walk now.
All is well.

# Graves' Web

Graves' web still winding me in;
Words drawn sharp from lexicon's scabbard
To protect a gentle soul.
Language inspired retreat
From the front line of emotions' war
In fields of joy and dread.
Literary surgery removes the exposed feelings;
Nerves under a poet's scalpel
In crème brûlée fields of winters' crunch.
On flow-stemming freeze
Poppied amputees dying for a warming word,
A single thread of shyness
Needled through the chest of man and boy
Held fast in the thickened scar.

# I Frightened Them

I frightened them,
They told me on the morning
She gave birth.
New Year's Day and time to spoil
The specialness in early spite.
No celebration here as I am sidelined.
Not central to the parental gift
Playing out.
More than one bottle of *Crofts*;
Hardly original
To be pissed before noon
Out of my mind
In the resentful clutch-fist of expectation.
How dare they,
Those who see the change in my eyes,
Who ought to hold me
In the centre of their day and every thought,
Live lives and harbour hopes
Independent of mine?
Love drowned by the jealous tide.
A reality divorced in vain striving to control
Every grain on the shifting beach.
My arms grew heavy;
I could not breathe under water.

# Patrisio

Soul consoling Patrisio.
Daffodil church crested on time's reverence,
Steeped in footpath faith.
Door forever open to the traveller
Chasing steeples to David's West,
Resting on your congregation
In stained light, screen and altar
Delicate sanctuary for those who search
Along hilltop lines.
Views over forests marked on walker's guides.
They sit in historic welcome,
Discerning somehow
What they may have meant
When they built it here.

# School Yard Select

Funny - the only way to win this game
Is not to play.
Decline the whistle's invitation
To begin the kicking.
Surrender ahead the knockout blow,
The jabbing against the ropes.
Throw in the stained towel.
Stay out of the brawl;
Bar yourself from entering the frayed
Edge of a deciding leg.
Brush off blizzard recall
Of backs against the wall of the playground,
Selection and deselection
In the hands of infant captains
Bristling with a natural malice;
Displaying an early, easy detachment.
Warnings, soundings of illimitable, crippling,
Powerless need.
Stay out of the game -
Spontaneity screams in its scarred shyness.

# Stalker

Dark hawk circling my longing.
Blue-bottled barfly
Frying on the hot trap,
Drawn from street's seclusion.
Hopper's colour fading.
Coffee-cold stepping out
In fog-breath free of the overhung,
Vine-dense crave of the morning.
My lamplight stalker stirs.
Sauntering threat in languid limber.
Silence draws on light's memory
In black and white abstinent dryness.

# Stay Off It

*How can I make amends, Son?*

*Just stay off the booze, Dad.*

*How can I say sorry, Sister?*

*Just stay off the booze, Brother.*

*How can I make it up to you, Mam?*

*Just stay off the booze, Love.*

*How can I capture lost time, Dad?*

*Just stay off the booze, Boy.*

*How can I be a husband, Darling?*

*Just stay off the booze, Darling.*

*How can I repay you, God?*

*Just stay off the booze, Child.*

# Swan

Cygnet-soft she drops through the hail wind.
Harboured debris parts under her webbed breeze.

Her runway in the calling cove.

No drogue, just ancient instinct
Deep in natural bank and response
In her necked-wing adjustments.

Angles made soft over the carrion bay,
She fore, and He aft,
Their armada of grey down dependence.

She lifts heavy in the tidal morning;
Wings waking the shore
In their audible struggle to the receiving sky.

# Straight the Way

Straight the way from Salisbury to the Preseli Hills;
Stones somehow shifted under history's weight.

Place and time gather in their circling,
Ancient beyond hints of light on solstice lines.

Rocks in bardic artistry weave a stanzaed thread
From the moon fathering stars to a mothered earth.

Bouldering awnings to rituals from Tinkinswood
To the fort downs of their crossed sanctuary wanderings.

Pebble towers from Pen-y-Fan to Snowdon:
Steeple-chasing prophecy of time searching futures.

Stories told under rock and water in cross-carve wordings,
Leaving monuments to stand in their infinite mystery.

# The Blank Page

Eyes raised from screen's blankness
Drawn through cut glazed morning,
Swells gently massaging the tired arms
Of the new mooring river.
Pristine mist in the yawning reeds.
Herons oblivious to drifting swans
Skating gently the stretching tide.
Pull back through vased rose
Opened velvet droplet held in thorn flowering
Of the hanging dawn.
New watered day on the table of my words,
The river trees have me in their grasp.
As the cormorant,
Confident in its disinterest
Lifts off the bored water,
Words begin their return,
Hopeful they may fly today
Across the skein sky of the waiting page.

# Taff

Taff flowing clear now under the pennants
By the arena of sporting kings and princes
To the new tigered bay.
Trout returning, the revolutionary river
Sourced in beacon tumbling through fawr and fechan,
Runs its wasteland
Drawing memories streaming from the slurried hills.
Elusive saplings above Aberfan
Looking out for them perhaps
Across the slow bend scar;
It mourns its respectful way to the story-telling sea.
Beyond the stillness of the pools at Nantgarw
Where the fish-fly ripples wink to the red castle,
She saunters bemused,
Picking her way through the shallow marinas
Slowing her ageless course to the bridled bay.

# The Lion

The Lion clawed my cirrhotic scales
To expose the life un-breathed.
Disrobed me at the mountain lake
And at its font bequeathed
Wine and song and daily bread
For journeys yet unmade;
Immersed me in the crystal pools
Then at His feet I laid.
In His eyes He led me through
The forest of my story
In the darkest woods of my selfish fears
To face my gnarled vainglory.
Across the night His voice unfurled
Both terrible and tender
And in His blood-stained paws I wept
A deep and slow surrender.
I woke amongst the skins I'd shed
In overwhelming loss
And rose to find the Lion's pelt
Stretched tight on makeshift cross.
I traced the prints in new fall snow
Drawn to pain's reunion.

On the hill where the golden Lion strode
They knelt in deep communion.
He roared the mountain land alive;
Love's sacramental birth.
We eat of the fruit and drank from the streams
And walked His receiving Earth.
At night's departing he called us come
To the stone's eternal greeting.
He laid His paws on weary heads
And blessed the holy meeting.
Keep coming back in willing reflection,
In unity, service, and prayer.
To hear the story He told from His cross,
To hear the Lion's Share.

# Dad

I was a good Dad, though?
We did father / son things?
Sorry for all this trouble and waste of your time.
All this hospital stuff
Surgeries and clinics.
I parked the car, took his hand, and said I loved him.
What else was there for me
On this quiet morning
But to be in the company of my father?
And now that I was out
And down from pedestaled
Son-hood I would say the words that wanted saying.
It was good to be back
Shameful yet to be back
Close to the veined and blue-boned hands that showed me how
To break in the willow
And hit from in to out
So my drives would draw and run on the springy turf.
Corn-Du and Pen-y-Fan
Deep backdrop to the first
Where, on hoar-crisp, even blue Boxing Day mornings,
Click it off the sweet spot.

Spiked shoe prints in the crunch,
Throwing the bags across our nonchalant shoulders
We strode out to the brow
Send our seconds soaring
To the flagged white circling
Where our putts made birdies,
Leaving their tall tale arcs
In the accepting frost.
I switched off the engine and told him I loved him.
Likewise; quiet and soft
Not risking eye contact.
Not the *I love you* that will make me feel better
When you are dead and gone.
But that which is here now
In the moment of shared and enduring calling.
No addictive control
That kept me at arm's length
For too long in the morn drunk, bottle-necked, prayer-less,
Barren gardened headland
Where the whole world owed me
New flowering entitlement of riches.
To sit with you patient,
Another waiting room.
Outbursts absent, nor strident complaining demands,
May be the web of change
That recovery weaves.

# Mam

In your profound forgetfulness
You remember home.
Strong calling from the stones;
Their dawn clouded in vascular storms.
The tidal ebb of yesterday
Drawing each memorial grain
Along ischaemic rivers to the blood clot sea.
Under the same roof you hold hands briefly,
Until you ask where you are and think of home again.
The company of strangers, fickle in its comfort,
Offers no challenge
To a lounge lonely yet familiar in its deep etch trace.
Sanctuary in mind's mists you live in blackout;
Empathy's unexpected maturing.
Continuity lifted from under your nose
By dementia's pickpockets
Leaving no thread weaving joy or security.
Walls erected between breakfast and lunch
In palpable transience.
My admiration hidden in the busyness.
My love unspoken in the midst of care.

*Patrisio Church*
*Patrisio, Grwyne Fawr Valley*
*Brecon Beacons*

# Faith

Courage to choose faith in doubt's stead.
To believe in God over the world,
In a world snapping its sinews to grind my folly.
Yet doubt I shall, for without its curious eye
Faith would be as a fearless courage.
Quiet visits where restlessness reigned;
Prayerful contact a conscious discernment of His will
In the clouds of a selfish mind.
Belief made real in palpable shifts in outlook
Possible only in a soul renewed.
Immersed in the language of fellowship
New vocabularies emerge,
Enabling shared experience as hope's foundation.
Joy surprises – its spontaneous arrival weaving trace
Of scene, colour, or touch,
Beyond reach and understanding,
A longing for the very essence of things
In frame or chord; personal encounters
Where youth and maturity become one
In timeless recognition of their enduring.
To know a presence as real as love.
Trust replaces insidious doubt; acceptance grows
In the space created by prayer.
Respect and tenderness dowse the empty plain
Of self-centred fear and rage; doing for me
What I could not do for myself.

And through surrender to the Spirit,
Through simple recognition of the searching,
The natural endless knowing and not knowing
First expressed in the art of caves,
Knowledge forges hope.
Blind faith could not work for me
In a land of cyclopean atheists.
History and ritual converge in sacrament.
On my knees I eat and drink of the body of man
In a moment of informed belief;
Intellect and spirit,
Where myth emerges as the means,
Imagination the creative spark to light a mere glimpse
Of the eternal.

ND - #0129 - 270225 - C0 - 229/152/3 - PB - 9781911265078 - Gloss Lamination